HONESTLY

HONESTLY

Hurting and Healing in Love

BRIANA CLEARLY

Honestly copyright © 2018 Briana Clearly. All Rights Reserved.

www.brianaclearly.com

ISBN: 978-1732212800

Published by The Gleaux House

A book dedicated to:

Those who choose love. Because of and in spite of...

HONESTLY

adverb hon·est·ly \ ˈä-nəst-lē \

Definition:

1 : in an honest manner: such as

    a : without cheating

    b : really, genuinely

    c : without frills

2 : to be honest : to tell the truth

Merriam-Webster's Dictionary

CONTENTS

OUT ON A LIMB — 9

HOLDING ON — 21

SUSPENDED — 33

LETTING GO — 43

WISDOM REARS ITS LOVELY HEAD — 59

OUT ON A LIMB

I wish I could have more courage. More confidence. I wish I could live beyond the fear. I wish I could've been more vulnerable while I was standing in front of you. But I'm a pussy and I'm scared as fvkk to tell you that I like you. That you move me. And it's because my fear of rejection is greater than my fear of the unknown. I'm too fragile. And I'm not prepared to hear you say that you don't like me. I also don't want to put pressure on you. I want us to still be us. Still create. Still laugh. Still be friends. But if I'm going to be your friend, the friend you deserve, I gotta keep it a buck. That means telling the truth about how I feel, regardless of whether it's reciprocated or not. So this is me, doing that. Saying that I like you, and cringing every step of the way.

iMessage 2LL120517 Revised

I inhale my future and exhale you. You seep from my pores.

Make me thirsty.

Words fell from my lips like razor blades.

Now a n*gga bleed for you. What do you have to say?

I freed myself from the weight of my own feelings just to be burdened by the weight of not knowing if they were mutual. Not sure which is heavier.

I'm so insecure.

Never quite sure of where I stand

Or how he feels about me.

Does he like me?

Yeah he calls back,

But he don't ever call.

Never. Not at all.

That's got to mean something, right?

I instinctively think the worst.

Lurking, searching for...

Proof, maybe.

Hurt I almost certainly find.

But sometimes, nothing.

It's just me, my mind.

The line between paranoia and intuition

Is extremely fine,

And I'm teetering between both sides.

Situationship

I'm plagued by the need to know. The need to understand.

It drives me mad.

I think a lot. Sometimes too much. And I analyze everything. I'm too hard on myself. And too easy on others. Mainly just guys. But, only the ones I like. And they take it for granted. They take me for granted. Damn! I'm too nice! I can't be mean! At least not to the peop---correction, the guys that deserve it.

The funny thing though, is that, when I'm an asshole. They like me. As soon as I show that I care, they don't. The fudge?! I get it, but I really don't. It's the game, but daggone, when does it end?

I'm saying. I can play. And I like to play. But at some point.

I don't wanna play anymore. I wanna be honest. Tell the truth. The whole truth. I wanna speak my mind. But I don't. I don't speak up because.

I don't wanna seem. I don't wanna seem clingy or naggy or bitchy or jealous. I wanna show strength. But I'm too scared. I'm scared to walk away or say no because. I want to be wanted. Sometimes so bad that. I ignore myself. My inside that says, "Let it go!"

Instead, I get run over. By a guy. Like a fool. I think sometimes I like to play the fool. I do it really well. It's bad! But I keep doing it! I wish I could be how I am when I'm with my friends. I don't care. I'm free. I can say whatever. I can do whatever. And be accepted. Be loved. Be understood. Be comforted. Be forgiven

But it doesn't happen that way. I stoop. I dumb down. I keep quiet. I compromise. I compromise myself. Just to be liked. Just to be wanted.

I thought he was it

The perfect person for me

He didn't agree

Haiku 12061702

I don't want to be strong or be okay. I want to be chosen.

HOLDING ON

I don't want you. Not because I don't want you, but because I don't want who you are to me. I deserve to be treated better. I deserve better. I'm better than what you give. You've given more hurt than joy. More pain than peace. You've broken me down into pieces. Leaving me to piece me back together when you leave me. Giving me only pieces of you when I'm giving my whole self. I've given my whole self and still. It's not enough.

I just want some love

Just a little affection

Reciprocity

Haiku 92317

I stand before you.

Naked, bare.

I bore my soul,

Pulled my heart out of my chest for you.

What more can I do?

Stretched my arms and my legs wide.

Parted my thighs like the Red Sea.

Fixed my eyes to see only you.

I love you.

I love only you.

Plant your seeds in my garden

Let me water them.

Plant your pains in my womb.

Let me absolve them.

Set you free so that

You're free to love me.

As I do you.

Pull off your cloak

Of pride.

Let go of your ego.

Let go.

Show me you.

Show me you within.

Let me into you.

Let me in.

How can you see me

Crying, hurting over you

And not feel a thing

Haiku 8151701

Trying to combat these bad thoughts. Thoughts of insufficiency, insecurity. Thoughts that I'm not good enough. That no one wants me. I'm a mess. I'm a fool. But I'm cool too. And…I love. I accept. I forgive. Isn't that good? Isn't that good enough?

Why don't you love me

Am I not enough for you

Maybe vice versa

Haiku 50617

...I wish you could've stayed around longer.

Instead you left me. Longing for you. And there's nothing I can do to change it. Now my heart is left hanging in the balance. All jumbled up from how you rearranged it.

Dear Jon Excerpt 32312

I'm the butt of every joke that love tells.

I've been chasing love

And have yet to catch that shit

I'm tired as fvkk

Haiku 80217

SUSPENDED

My biggest fear. Greatest fear. Is loneliness. Eternal loneliness. And I get closer to realizing it everyday.

Every rejection chips away at the goodness of my heart.

I wonder. How much will be left for the one that accepts me?

I'm sad more days than I'm comfortable admitting.

I'm more sensitive than is socially acceptable.

I don't feel safe. I don't feel safe to love.

Doing things I said I'd never do again,

With people I said I'd never see again.

Bad decisions make the best stories.

I feel…I don't know…like…not…a little…off, maybe…weird.

Not myself…not quite…not as good as I normally do. It'll pass.

It's just a phase. I hope.

I think there's a misconception that confidence is concrete. That you either have it or you don't. But I don't think that's really true. I think confidence can be, and is, situational. I think it's absolutely possible to be confident in one aspect of life, and completely insecure in another.

Honesty saves time

But we waste so much on lies

Lies must taste sweeter

Haiku 50517

LETTING GO

If I were to tell you anything, I'd say...I've told you everything. I don't want to keep repeating myself. I don't want to keep proving myself. I just want to be valued and wanted and respected and cared for and loved. Like a human being. Like a woman. Like a good woman. Like the great woman that I am. And maybe you can't do that. And I have to accept that. And give myself to someone who can. Because I deserve that. I'm worth all that and more... Sometimes I want that to be you, but there's a good chance it may not be. Such is life.

Things I Can't Say To You

You could be the love of my life,

That don't make you right for me.

As much as we would fight,

How could this be life for me?

I've become my worst while looking for you to see the best in me.

I've held onto the first night we ever spent together for almost eight months.

This is how irrational love is; it doesn't have to be based in something incredibly deep or substantial. It can simply be rooted in a fantasy that has been created by the desires of the heart.

I now find myself where I've been more times than I care to remember. Picking the pieces of my heart off the floor. Restoring my dignity and self worth.

Coming to terms with the fact that you don't want me or care for me the way I wish you would. Trying to be alright with having made a fool of myself by chasing a man that doesn't want to be caught by me. And it's hard. All of it.

I'm having a one sided conversation to get some semblance of closure. I'm writing a letter to accept an apology I may never receive.

I have to manage the delicate balance of understanding you're not right for me without feeling like you're a horrible person and hating you. I just want to be over you, so I can make room for someone who wants to love me the way I need.

I'm so done with you

The end been long overdue

Better now than not

Haiku 81417

It's been less than a week

And I miss you.

I wanna call you, but nah,

I can't even.

Even though I chose me,

I don't feel as free as I thought I would.

It don't feel as good as I thought it would.

But no one ever said doing what's best

Would be easy.

I did the right thing,

But it seems like

I made a mistake.

In my mind I know I had to take certain steps

Away from you.

I was too close.

In my heart I wasn't close enough,

Too far away from you.

And I know you.

I know you took it personal.

I know I hurt you.

I apologize.

My intent was not to make you feel less than

But to tell you I need more than you can or want to give.

And it's okay.

I'm okay with that.

But I can't just wait.

And fall deeper.

And wait.

And love harder.

And wait.

Instead, I choose me.

And maybe,

One of these days

You'll see.

I did the right thing.

Do The Right Thing

It's over for him

No matter what he tells you

Don't ever go back

Haiku 8221701

When your vagina gets curved cuz God had to intervene cuz he had to save you from partaking in hoe-ish ways with fvkk boys cuz you gotta watch ya back cuz you not just anybody.

He fill my womb.

You fill my thoughts.

He on top of me while

You on my top.

I cry internally

Because he on top of me,

And you on my top.

I want to say stop, but

I'm hoping he can stroke the thoughts of you away.

He stroke.

I'm so far away.

With you.

Somewhere far away.

From here.

From him.

And he no one new,

But now he hurt.

My heart hurt

Because of you.

Because he not you.

Pain in my womb.

He moan.

He feel at home

In my womb.

He was once invited in,

But now he feel estranged

From my womb.

I hope he come soon.

Please come soon,

Won't you?

Come back soon.

I say to myself.

I say to you.

As I lie here.

Away from him.

Away from you.

I can heal myself

I just need to cry sometimes

Get it out. Love on. (Move on)

Haiku 10161701

I've planted my fingers and toes into the dirt. Sunken into the soil. The coldness makes me shiver. The moistness makes me tingle. And I feel myself growing. I feel myself. Grow. I feel. I grow.

For a long time, I was fighting between wanting to be with you and letting you go, loving you and hating you. I've now realized that I can love you without wanting or needing anything from you. I can love you and still move on from you. You can be a positive passing thought rather than a negative, or draining, lingering one.

I no longer have expectations of you. I pass no judgment, nor do I seek compromise.

I extend friendship, understanding, support, and unconditional love without worry of whether you accept it or not because it is not a request, it's merely an invitation.

If this is the last we ever speak, I want you to have everything that's for you. I only speak life, love, and happiness over you. I forgive you for everything. I thank you for everything. I love you.

I just realized. I manifested it.

You loving me. But I forgot.

I didn't specify when. And now. You love me.

And I no longer need it. But thank you anyway.

WISDOM REARS ITS LOVELY HEAD

I've always felt like love wasn't good to me,

But maybe I just wasn't good to myself.

Habits are formed and broken by the minute, not by the day.

Contrary To Popular Belief

Pain can feel good if applied to the right places.

The heart is not one of them.

Pussy be magic

Pussy give life to the Earth

Pussy God for real

Haiku 072017

Avoid the grey. The abyss. The space where someone feels free to disrespect you, hurt you, abuse you and not be held accountable.

Transformed my "Ls" into elevation.

Never go backwards

Use the past as reference

But do not dwell there

Haiku 8221702

Don't sweat the small stuff. It's not your job to prove yourself. It's your job to be yourself. Don't be so critical of who you are. Others do that enough. Learn to recognize your gifts and love your flaws. Love yourself. Love yourself so much that someone else will have no choice but to love you as much as you love yourself, and that better be at the very least. Love yourself to the point where you refuse to settle. Know the difference between settling and compromising. Set high standards, but not impossible ones. Set standards for yourself and work toward meeting them. Set standards for others that you want in your life. Put forth the type of energy and aura that attracts those with the qualities you look for.

You've had to fight to become who you are. To accept who you are. To love who you are. And you will have to continue to fight for yourself everyday. But anything worth having is worth fighting for.

Look to find balance

Between wits and believing

Your gut will guide you

Haiku 90917

The difference between being broken and being bent

Is the ability to be flexible.

Love. Inhale. Love. Exhale. Love.

Second Nature

www.ingramcontent.com/pod-product-compliance
Lightning Source LLC
Chambersburg PA
CBHW070631050426
42450CB00011B/3162